# Tim Tebow
## A Football Star Who Cares

Ken Rappoport

**Enslow Elementary**

an imprint of

**Enslow Publishers, Inc.**

40 Industrial Road
Box 398
Berkeley Heights, NJ 07922
USA

http://www.enslow.com

Enslow Elementary, an imprint of Enslow Publishers, Inc.

Enslow Elementary® is a registered trademark of Enslow Publishers, Inc.

**Library of Congress Cataloging-in-Publication Data**

Rappoport, Ken.
    Tim Tebow : a football star who cares / Ken Rappoport.
       p. cm. — (Sports stars who care)
    Includes bibliographical references and index.
    ISBN 978-0-7660-4297-1
    1. Tebow, Tim, 1987—Juvenile literature 2. Football players—United States—Biography—Juvenile
literature. I. Title.
    GV949.T423R37 2013
    796.332092—dc23
    [B]                     2012041573

Future Editions:
Paperback ISBN: 978-1-4644-0539-6
EPUB ISBN: 978-1-4645-1275-9
Single-User PDF ISBN: 978-1-4646-1275-6
Multi-User PDF: 978-0-7660-5907-8

Printed in the United States of America

052013 Lake Book Manufacturing, Inc., Melrose Park, IL

10 9 8 7 6 5 4 3 2 1

**To Our Readers:** We have done our best to make sure all Internet addresses in this book were active and appropriate when we went to press. However, the author and the Publisher have no control over, and assume no liability for, the material available on those Internet sites or on other Web sites they may link to. Any comments or suggestions can be sent by e-mail to comments@enslow.com or to the address on the back cover.

♻ Enslow Publishers, Inc., is committed to printing our books on recycled paper. The paper in every book contains 10% to 30% post-consumer waste (PCW). The cover board on the outside of each book contains 100% PCW. Our goal is to do our part to help young people and the environment too!

**Illustration Credits:** AP Images/April L. Brown, p. 29; AP Images/Ben Margot, p. 33; AP Images/Eric Bakke, p. 39; AP Images/G. Newman Lowrance, p. 12; AP Images/Jack Dempsey, pp. 11, 35; AP Images/John Raoux, p. 18; AP Images/Julie Jacobson, p. 25; AP Images/Julio Cortez, p. 4; AP Images/Lynne Sladky, pp. 1, 30; AP Images/ Mel Evans, p. 40; AP Images/Phil Sandlin, pp. 21, 23; AP Images/Reinhold Matay, p. 27; AP Images/Rick Wilson, p. 17; AP Images/Scott A. Miller, pp. 8, 36; AP Images/*The Denver Post*/John Leyba, p. 6; AP Images/*The Florida Times-Union*/Bruce Lipsky, p. 15; AP Images/*The Florida Times-Union*/Kelly Jordan, p. 42.

**Cover Illustration:** AP Images/Lynne Sladky

# Contents

# Introduction

**B**efore Tim Tebow had played a down in the NFL, he was already one of the most popular players in the game.

He also was one of the most discussed figures in football. Love him or hate him, Tebow had inspired an enormous amount of attention. He had as many critics as he had fans.

Everyone was waiting to see how Tebow would perform in the pros following his success in college. He had won the Heisman Trophy and played on two national championship teams with the Florida Gators.

He brought unusual talents to the quarterback position. He was a double threat because he could run as well as pass. Usually pro quarterbacks rely mostly on throwing the ball or handing it off to a running back. Tebow was not expected to succeed in the NFL. His style was not in the tradition of the great quarterbacks. Throughout his career in high school, college, and professional football, Tebow was told he could not succeed.

But Tebow's dedication and faith made him think otherwise.

So meet Tim Tebow, one of the most interesting football players you will ever know.

**Tebow launches a pass in a game against the Chicago Bears.**

**T**im Tebow faced the biggest challenge of his career.

The Denver Broncos quarterback was in a tailspin. The team had three straight losses to end the 2011 NFL regular season. Now it was the playoffs. His dream job of quarterbacking an NFL team was on the line.

## Chapter 1

# Mile High

**Tim Tebow watches the scoreboard clock tick down at the end of a come-from-behind win during the 2011 season.**

Tebow needed to reach deep within himself. He felt personally responsible for the losses. He was determined to work harder than he ever had. He did not want to let his teammates down. It was time for prayer.

For a time in the 2011 season, Tebow was unbeatable. He had come off the bench to lead the Broncos to six straight victories. The streak had moved the Broncos to the top of the AFC West division. If they stayed atop their division, they would make the playoffs.

But with Tebow at the helm, the Broncos had closed out the regular season with three straight losses. They finished with an 8–8 record and just barely made it into the playoffs.

Many had lost faith in the young quarterback. Was his six-game winning streak just lucky?

Tebow had been regarded as a risk to play in the NFL. Pro quarterbacks were strong in the passing game. 'Tebow couldn't pass.' That was what critics were saying about him. It was the one essential element for a quarterback in the pros. But Tebow's passing percentage was the lowest among the NFL's starting quarterbacks.

Tebow saw himself as a double-threat player; part quarterback and part running back. His game relied heavily on his ability as a runner. The powerfully built 6-foot-3, 240-pound Tebow often chalked up as much yardage with his runs as with his passing.

Different? Yes, but no one could deny his faith on and off the field. He was a hot topic and a fan favorite wherever he had played: high school, college, or the pros.

Son of a missionary, Tebow's deeply religious convictions had drawn attention to him. He could often be seen kneeling on the sidelines in prayer in what has become known as "Tebowing."

≈ ≈ ≈ ≈ ≈

Tebow awoke on the morning of his first playoff game. One of the first things he did was reach for his iPhone. For his fans on Facebook and Twitter, he keyed "Hebrews 12:1-2", a message from the Bible.

"I've always loved that verse because it's very encouraging ..." Tebow said. "It talks about having

Tim Tebow kneels down and prays before the start of the second half of a game against the New England Patriots. Kneeling in this way has been called "Tebowing."

endurance—whether it's endurance in your faith or endurance as we play a game."

Awaiting the underdog Broncos were the Pittsburgh Steelers, one of the NFL's elite franchises. They had won a record six Super Bowls and boasted a league-high defense during the 2011 season.

Game time!

Demaryius Thomas streaks down the sideline to complete an 80-yard touchdown pass.

Tebow filled the air with footballs. In the second quarter alone, Tebow completed passes of 51, 30, and 58 yards.

Then came the topper in overtime. Just eleven seconds into the extra period, Tebow threw an 80-yard pass to Demaryius Thomas.

Touchdown!

It was the quickest overtime touchdown in NFL playoff history.

Broncos win, 29–23.

Tebow finished with a career-high 316 passing yards. He threw for two touchdowns, and scored another on the ground. He answered his critics who said he couldn't pass.

An excited Tebow jumped into the stands, slapping high-fives with fans. Then he fell on one knee in prayer.

His early life had prepared him for such a moment.

It was hot and the doctors were tired. There were still long lines outside the clinic in a remote area of the Philippines. So many people needed medical treatment.

Tim Tebow was ready to help. From the time he turned fifteen, Tim worked as a missionary with his father. Helping to assist the doctors was not unusual for Tim.

## Chapter 2

# Making a Difference

"They were teaching us how to do things, so I really was performing surgeries," Tebow said. "I couldn't do that (in the United States), but I really did it there."

Tebow was born in the Philippines on August 14, 1987. He is the son of missionary parents. Missionaries travel to remote areas of the world to provide much needed medical and dental treatment.

Making a difference in people's lives was ingrained in his upbringing and very important to Tim. His other love was football. His dream was to become a quarterback.

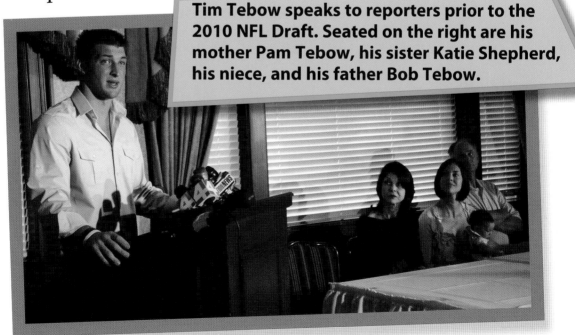

Tim Tebow speaks to reporters prior to the 2010 NFL Draft. Seated on the right are his mother Pam Tebow, his sister Katie Shepherd, his niece, and his father Bob Tebow.

"Tim Tebow was different." That is what they said. He wanted to be a quarterback. Coaches thought he looked more like a linebacker, tackle, or tight end; not a quarterback. So growing up, Tim ended up mostly playing those positions. Tim called it a position by stereotype.

That did not mean he was not an offensive force. At age eleven, he was on the Lakeshore Renegades in Jacksonville, Florida. There was a problem. The Renegades were losing games. What did the coach do? He changed the system he had been using for many years. He structured his offense around Tebow. He spread out the offense and let Tebow use his varied talents.

"We designed plays just for him that we used," said Renegades coach David Hess.

The team went to the regional championship.

Tim attended the Trinity Christian Academy, a high school in Jacksonville. Tebow again faced an obstacle. Because of his super-size build, Tebow played nose tackle, linebacker, and tight end. But he

Tim Tebow celebrates with lineman Doug Polochak after Nease High School won the 2005 state championship.

still wanted to be a quarterback. He wondered if he should change schools.

The coach at Nease High School in Ponte Vedra, Florida was willing to give him that chance. But the team had not had a winning campaign in ten years.

Critics said it would be a dumb decision. But Tebow never listened to critics. He changed schools.

17

Coach Craig Howard was using the "spread offense" that allowed the quarterback to create plays. Howard also liked a high-powered passing game.

Tebow struggled at first. Nease lost five of its last six games in his sophomore year. By his second season, Tebow helped turn the program around. As a senior, he led the Panthers to the state championship.

Former high school teammates Tebow and wide receiver Austin Silvoy (right) shake hands after a game between their colleges. Florida beat Troy University, 59–31.

He was voted Florida's Mister Football for the second straight year.

"To turn that program around . . . that was one of the proudest moments I ever had in sports," Tebow said.

With his double-threat ability to run and pass, Tebow was one of the most exciting high school players in Florida. He was starting to get national attention as well. Everyone wanted to see him play.

His mental toughness matched his physical toughness. As a sophomore, he suffered a broken leg in one game, but nevertheless kept on playing.

"It wasn't a crack, it was a definite broken leg with a jagged bone," Howard recalled. "Right then I knew he was the toughest son of a gun I'd ever seen in my life."

Tebow had been great in high school. But would his football style work in college?

It was decision day for Tim Tebow.

He was recruited by dozens of college football teams. Now he had narrowed the choices to two schools. The announcement would be made in a national news conference. But on the day before, he still had not made up his mind. Would it be the Florida Gators or the Alabama Crimson Tide?

## Chapter 3

# Hello, Heisman

Freshman Tim Tebow attends his first media day on the Florida campus.

Growing up, Tebow was a fan of the Florida football team. But he had a friendship with Mike Shula, then the head coach at the University of Alabama. Which team would he choose?

On December 13, 2005, Tim stood before the ESPN microphones. It was time to choose. Tebow was going to Florida.

There were still critics. There were questions if he could succeed on the college level. But it did not take long for Tebow to adapt. As a freshman in 2006, he played a key role behind starter Chris Leak. That season, Florida faced LSU in a battle of national championship contenders.

There was less than a minute in the first half when Tebow trotted onto the field. The ball was on LSU's one-yard line with the score tied 7–7.

In the huddle Tebow called the play: "jump pass." The Gators broke the huddle. Tebow received the ball from center and took off toward the end zone. Suddenly he stopped and jumped high at the 2. He flipped a pass to tight end Tate Casey. Touchdown!

It was the kind of pass shown in old football movies. Leave it to Tim Tebow. His first touchdown pass was different. The Gators went into the dressing room with a 14–7 lead. They went on to beat LSU 23–10 on the way to the national championship.

Tebow took over the starting role in his second year in college. Tebow did it all for the Gators in the 2007 season. Florida won its first four games to start the season.

Freshman quarterback Tim Tebow bursts through LSU's linemen for a key gain in a game on October 7, 2006.

Then the team lost three out of the next four contests. The Gators were out of the national championship picture. But Tebow was still piling up huge numbers.

A Heisman Trophy candidate? Tebow was only a sophomore. In the seventy-three-year history of the Heisman, a sophomore had never won the award. Did he have a chance?

Late in the season, Florida faced South Carolina. The Gators were in trouble. One of their top players was sidelined by illness.

Tebow came to the rescue. He responded with one of his greatest performances: five touchdown runs and two TD passes in a 51–31 rout of the Gamecocks.

It was a great performance. Did it clinch the Heisman Trophy for Tebow?

Tebow had put together a staggering season: nearly 4,000 yards of total offense and 51 touchdowns. He became the first major college player to throw for at least 20 touchdowns and run for 20 in a single season.

It was time for the Heisman ceremony in New York City. Tebow sat in the front row with the other candidates. They were all anxious as they awaited the decision.

When his name was announced as the winner, Tebow was excited. He jumped up, ran to his parents, and gave them a big hug. He hugged his coach too.

"It's overwhelming, I'm kind of at a loss for words," Tebow said.

With one prize under his belt, Tebow set his sights on another: the national championship.

Could he do it as a junior?

Tim Tebow won the Heisman Trophy during his amazing 2007 sophomore season.

**T**im Tebow, Superman?

That was his nickname on the University of Florida campus.

With Tebow leading the way, the Gators had smashed Hawaii, the University of Miami, and Tennessee. They had outscored their opponents 112–19 in the first three games of the 2008 season.

# Chapter 4

# The Promise

But then they lost. It was a 31–30 loss to Ole Miss. Could they recover?

Tebow was upset with the loss. When he met the media, his voice cracked with emotion. He had hoped for an undefeated season. That hope was now gone.

He felt he had to apologize to the fans.

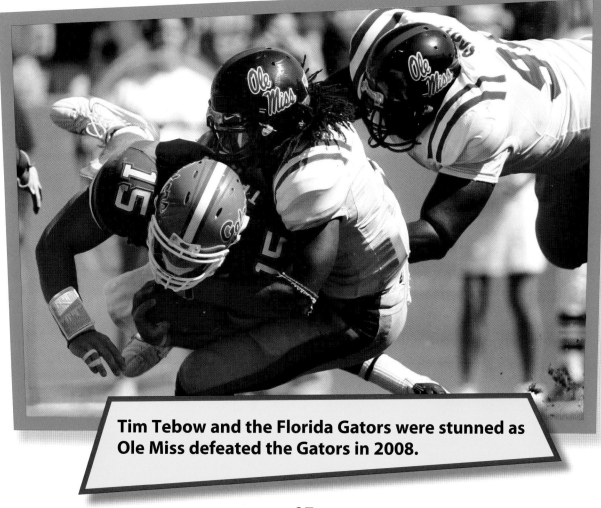

Tim Tebow and the Florida Gators were stunned as Ole Miss defeated the Gators in 2008.

"You will never see any player in the entire country play as hard as I will play the rest of the season," Tebow said. "You will never see someone push the rest of the team as hard as I will push everybody the rest of the season."

Tim's heartfelt apology became known at the University of Florida as "The Promise."

Next game, the Gators crushed Arkansas, 38–7. The next seven games were not even close. The Gators were on a hot streak on their way to the SEC title game. Their opponent: Alabama.

It was no problem. The Gators rolled past the Tide, 31–20.

Now it was No. 1 ranked Florida against No. 2 Oklahoma in the BCS title game. At stake: the national championship. The game featured a battle of Heisman Trophy winners: Tebow and Oklahoma's Sam Bradford.

Both quarterbacks struggled during the first two quarters. Except for a touchdown pass, Tebow was having a tough time getting the offense started. He was intercepted twice. At halftime, the teams went into the locker room tied 7–7.

"In the locker room, (Tebow) came up to us and apologized to us and blamed the first half on himself," said Gators wide receiver David Nelson. "That's something he didn't need to do, but he did. He's led us to victories all year."

Then came the second half against Oklahoma.

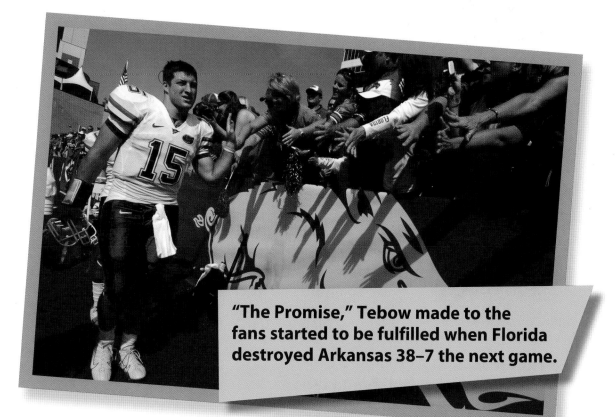

"The Promise," Tebow made to the fans started to be fulfilled when Florida destroyed Arkansas 38–7 the next game.

"You could tell, he just had a different approach, a different attitude in the second half," Nelson said.

Tebow drove Florida to a touchdown and a field goal to give the Gators a 17–14 lead late in the game. With less than four minutes left, the Gators had another opportunity to score.

**Tim Tebow scrambles to avoid being sacked by the tough Oklahoma defense in the BCS National Championship game.**

Tebow took a couple of hard steps toward the goal line as if to run. Suddenly, he stopped short, jumped, and fired a four-yard touchdown pass to Nelson with 3:07 left.

That sealed a 24–14 win for the Gators. It was their second national championship in three years. Tebow was voted the game's outstanding player. He had outplayed Bradford, who had beaten him out for that year's Heisman Trophy.

"Tebow, just call him Superman," said Gators running back Percy Harvin.

"The Promise" was remembered with a plaque outside Ben Hill Griffin Stadium, the Gators' home field.

Just call him Superman, indeed.

**K**eep the faith.

Since being drafted by the Denver Broncos in 2010, Tim Tebow was the subject of intense national scrutiny. Opinion was sharply divided. Could he make it in the pros with his unusual style of play? In a sports magazine poll of 111 NFL players, Tebow was voted the most overrated player in the league.

## Chapter 5

# Taking Off

After scoring a touchdown on a 40-yard run in his first NFL start, Tim Tebow made many fans believe he was going to be a star.

Tebow never stopped believing in himself.

"I'm going to work every day as hard as I can, one game at a time, one day at a time," he said.

The No. 1 quarterback for the Broncos? It was not Tebow. He was the backup to Kyle Orton. It was not until late in the 2010 season that Tebow finally got his first pro start. By this time, Denver had a record of 3–10.

On the way to a 39–23 road loss to the Oakland Raiders, Tebow scored on a 40-yard run. It was the longest touchdown run in NFL history by a quarterback in his first start.

One week later, a day after Christmas, Tebow made his first home start. But he was having a tough time. The Broncos fell behind the Houston Texans 17–0 at halftime. Could Tebow pull it out?

No problem. The Broncos outscored the Texans 24–6 in the second half. His six-yard touchdown run put Denver ahead for good. In the limited time that he quarterbacked the Broncos, Tebow showed sparks of brilliance.

Tebow was ready for the 2011 season. He was hoping to see more action. So were his fans. They chanted Tim Tebow's name at games. They rented a billboard in support of their hero. But Tebow once again began the season as Orton's backup.

It happened in the fifth game of the season. The Broncos trailed San Diego 23–10 at the half when Tebow replaced Orton. The fans roared their approval.

Tebow entered a 2010 game against the Texans with his team losing 17–0, and led Denver to a 24–23 victory. Tebow is shown barreling through the defense for a six-yard touchdown.

Tebow led the Broncos on two fourth-quarter touchdown drives. But his last-second pass for another touchdown fell short. The Broncos lost 29–24. But Tebow's play had impressed everyone.

Broncos coach John Fox was swayed. He made an announcement. Tebow was going to be his starting quarterback in the next game at Miami.

It was a big day for Tebow. He would be playing before his college coach, Urban Meyer. It was the

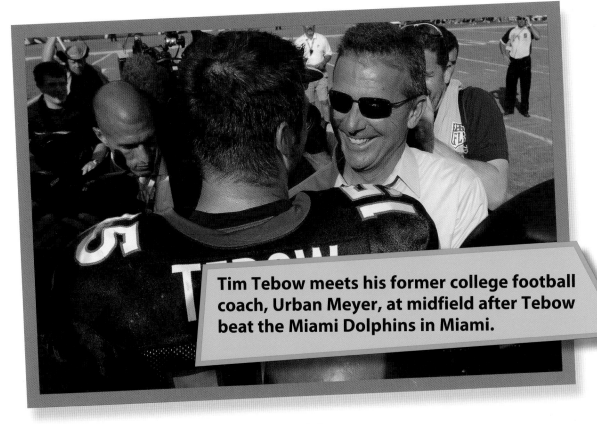

Tim Tebow meets his former college football coach, Urban Meyer, at midfield after Tebow beat the Miami Dolphins in Miami.

same stadium where he won the 2008 college national championship. Now was the time to shine.

But for fifty-five minutes, Tebow failed. He did not register a single point. The Broncos trailed one of the league's weakest teams, 15–0.

If Tebow was going to make a comeback, this would be a tough one. No team in NFL history had ever rallied from a 15-point deficit to win with three minutes left in a game.

But Tebow was not about to give up. His will to win was too strong. He fired two touchdown passes. After the second, with seventeen seconds left, he completed the two-point conversion. The game was now tied, 15–15. The Broncos beat the Dolphins by a field goal in overtime.

"Tebow turned into the player who inspires fans to erect billboards," wrote Judy Battista of *The New York Times*.

Could Tebow continue his success in the pros?

**N**ot so fast, Tim.

The miracle at Miami was long forgotten by the following week. Facing the Detroit Lions, Tebow was sacked an incredible seven times. The result: an embarrassing 45–10 loss for the Broncos.

Following the game, the Lions insulted the young quarterback. "Come on, that's your

## Chapter 6

# The Comeback Kid

quarterback? Seriously?" said a Detroit defensive player. The Lions players mocked the so-called "Tebowing" prayer pose that was so familiar to football fans.

The media joined in the insult parade. "Tebow is the worst quarterback in the NFL," said one reporter. Broncos coach John Fox was asked if Tebow was still

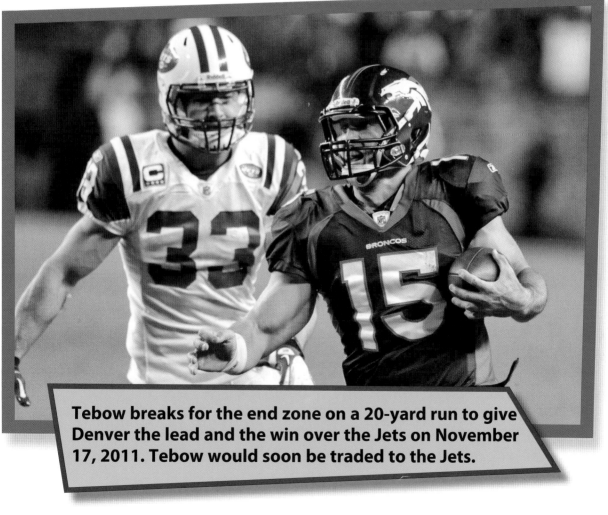

Tebow breaks for the end zone on a 20-yard run to give Denver the lead and the win over the Jets on November 17, 2011. Tebow would soon be traded to the Jets.

**Tim Tebow holds his first press conference as a New York Jet.**

the Broncos' starting quarterback. "For this week, yes," Fox replied.

Tebow would have to do a lot better against the Broncos next opponent if he hoped to keep his job. The following week, he did: Denver 38, Oakland 24. Tebow rushed for over 100 yards and threw two touchdown passes.

Next up was Kansas City. It ended with another victory for the Broncos. Tebow then guided the Broncos to wins over the New York Jets, San Diego Chargers, Minnesota Vikings, and Chicago Bears. Tebow made comebacks a habit. He rallied the Broncos back from deficits in the late going in four of those games.

Tebow's amazing play helped the Broncos win the AFC West title. Following an exciting victory over the Pittsburgh Steelers, the Broncos were knocked out of the playoffs by the New England Patriots.

Tebow's inspirational performances had raised his status in the eyes of the NFL. The league named him among its Top 100 players. It was especially impressive because he had been selected by his fellow players.

Soon there was big news involving Tebow: He was traded. In a deal that shook up the football world, he was now a New York Jet. A New York Jet with a mission.

His Tim Tebow Foundation teamed with another charitable foundation to build a children's hospital in the Philippines. "These children and their families are so poor, they can never hope to afford the type of care needed," Tebow said.

Tebow will travel anywhere to share his faith. He is not afraid of dangerous situations. He has traveled to prisons.

The Tim Tebow Foundation started opening Timmy's Playrooms. These are facilities that give children with life-threatening sicknesses a place to have fun.

"You're talking to guys who have no hope, no support, who have been written off by the world," Tebow said.

He speaks at schools and churches and before youth groups, stressing the importance of positive role models. It's one of his favorite things to do. His message: "Even when you're losing, when things aren't going right, don't give up. Keep working. Keep trying. Have faith."

"It's not what you do when you're up," Tebow says. "It's what you do when you're down."

Now with the Jets, Tebow was starting over with a new team. During the 2012 season he saw time at fullback, tight end, on special teams, and a little at quarterback. Mainly, he backed up starter Mark Sanchez. The Jets had a dreadful season and Tebow was released on April 29, 2013.

He had to prove himself all over again. But it was just another challenge for Tim Tebow. After all, he is no stranger to meeting challenges.

| College Football | | | | | | | | | | | |
|---|---|---|---|---|---|---|---|---|---|---|---|
| | | | Passing | | | | | Rushing | | | |
| Year | Team | Games | Att | Comp | Yds | TD | Int | Att | Yds | TD |
| 2006 | Florida | 14 | 33 | 22 | 358 | 5 | 1 | 89 | 469 | 8 |
| 2007 | Florida | 13 | 350 | 234 | 3,286 | 32 | 6 | 210 | 895 | 23 |
| 2008 | Florida | 14 | 298 | 192 | 2,746 | 30 | 4 | 176 | 673 | 12 |
| 2009 | Florida | 14 | 314 | 213 | 2,895 | 21 | 5 | 217 | 910 | 14 |
| | TOTALS | 55 | 995 | 661 | 9,285 | 88 | 16 | 692 | 2,947 | 57 |

| NFL | | | | | | | | | | | |
|---|---|---|---|---|---|---|---|---|---|---|---|
| | | | Passing | | | | | Rushing | | | |
| Year | Team | Games | Att | Comp | Yds | TD | Int | Att | Yds | TD |
| 2010 | Broncos | 9 | 82 | 41 | 654 | 5 | 3 | 43 | 227 | 6 |
| 2011 | Broncos | 14 | 271 | 126 | 1,729 | 12 | 6 | 122 | 660 | 6 |
| 2012 | Jets | 12 | 8 | 6 | 39 | 0 | 0 | 32 | 102 | 0 |
| | TOTALS | 35 | 361 | 173 | 2,422 | 17 | 9 | 197 | 989 | 12 |

Att = Attempts          Pct = Completion Percentage     TD = Touchdowns
Comp = Completions       Yds = Yards                     Int = Interceptions

# Where to Write

**TIM TEBOW**
**C/O TIM TEBOW FOUNDATION**
2220 County Road 210 W
Suite 108, PMB 317
Jacksonville, FL 32259

# Words to Know

**AFC**—American Football Conference.

**BCS**—Bowl Championship Series, various bowl games that decide the national football championship.

**Ben Hill Griffin Stadium**—Home of the Florida Gators.

**double-threat**—A player who can both pass and run.

**hand off**—A play in which the quarterback tucks the ball into the running back's midsection. The running back then tries to gain forward yardage.

**Hebrews**—In this text, Hebrews refers to the Letter to the Hebrews. This is a book in the New Testament of the Christian Bible.

**Heisman Trophy**—Awarded to the best college football player over one season.

**linebacker**—Position on the defense mainly tasked with stopping the opponents running backs.

**line of scrimmage**—The offense starts play at this line on the field.

**missionary**—People who travel and give aid to those less fortunate. They are often part of a religious group.

**NFC**—National Football Conference.

**NFL**—National Football League.

**passing percentage**—The number of a quarterback's attempts divided by the number of completed passes. Then that number is multiplied by 100.

**Philippines**—An island nation located in the Pacific Ocean off the southeastern coast of China.

**quarterback**—The player in charge of the offense.

**sack**—When the quarterback is tackled behind the line of scrimmage.

**SEC**—Southeastern Conference.

**sophomore**—Second year of college.

**spread offense**—A play that opens up the offense and allows the quarterback to be more creative.

**Super Bowl**—The NFL championship game.

**tackle**—Position in football. On offense, the tackles block. On defense, the tackles try to get to the quarterback.

**tailspin**—A long-lasting streak of negative events.

**"Tebowing"**—Modeled after Tim Tebow, the generally accepted practice of kneeling on the sidelines in prayer.

**tight end**—Position in football at the end of the offensive line. Most tight ends are mainly blockers, but they also can go out and catch passes.

## Books

Klis, Mike. *Tim Tebow A Promise Kept*. Hauppauge, New York: Barron's Educational Books, 2012.

Savage, Jeff. *Tim Tebow*. Minneapolis, Minn.: Lerner Publications Company, 2012.

Yorkey, Mike. *Playing with Purpose: Inside the Lives and Faith of Today's Biggest Football, Basketball, and Baseball Stars.* Uhrichsville, Ohio: Barbour Books, 2012.

## Internet Addresses

### Official Website of Tim Tebow
http://www.timtebow.com

### Official Site of Tim Tebow Foundation
http://www.timtebowfoundation.org

### Official Site of Florida Gators Football
http://www.gatorzone.com/football/

# Index